GREENER LIVING

MS. SUREKHA CHIDAMBARANATH

As an initiative of UNDP's Sustainable Development Goals 2030, MES's Pillai College of Education and Research, Chembur dedicates this book to encourage and foster green practices in the society.

Green practices

Contents

Table of Contents

I

Sustainability- It starts with You

Ms. Surekha Chidambaranath

Assistant Professor,
MES's Pillai College of Education and Research
Chembur, Mumbai.

> **"The greatest threat to our planet is the belief that someone else will save it."**
> **– Robert Swan, Author**

One sees a tap on the railway platform, from which water has been flowing continuously and thinks to himself, 'I am in a hurry, someone else will turn it off' and there is the choice that we make, to be negligent of what is going on around us.

We humans are completely reliant on the environment, and we know its value too, but still, we choose to exploit it thinking one person, in one corner of the world, doing something wrong is not going to affect the whole world.

Our world is facing a severe environmental crisis. Air pollution, water pollution, massive quantities of toxic waste, soil erosion and destruction of the ozone layer are those severe issues which are the effects of human intervention on the environment. Our forefathers were never concerned about the environment because those days the population was less, there were more trees and human settlements were quite basic. But as man got educated and smarter, his needs and wants became complex. In the process of creating appliances to make his work simpler, he harmed the environment without even realising what impact his actions had on it.

Recently, there has been an increase in mechanization, which is the use of equipment and machinery that are powered by fossil fuels with the aim of reducing the dependency on manual labour and to increase productivity, quality and efficiency. However, these machineries are also responsible for the issues pertaining to the environment and human health and safety.

The celebration of different festivals is what brings us closer, but lately, it seems to be doing the opposite of what it is supposed to be doing. Take Diwali for example. Diwali was called the festival of lights, where everyone would light oil lamps all around the house which represents luminance. The lamps are lit to dispel darkness not only from our houses but also from our lives (symbolically). There is no evidence as to how and when bursting crackers became a part of the celebrations. And over the years, the kinds of crackers that burst during the Diwali season have spiked the Air Quality Index from Good to Satisfactory.

Even though the fashion sector is booming, we cannot ignore the imposing negative environmental impacts that the industry is responsible for. Fashion production makes up 10% of humanity's carbon emissions, dries up water sources, and pollutes rivers and streams. What's more, 85% of all textiles go to the dump each year (UNECE, 2018), and washing some types of clothes sends a significant amount of microplastics into the ocean. The equivalent of one garbage truck full of clothes is burned or dumped in a landfill every second (UNEP, 2018).

Whatever food you eat also has an impact on the environment. Yes, you read it right. The modern farming techniques and agricultural practices cause air as well as water pollution. Production of food, livestock, and packaged food emit gases into the environment which are harmful for the environment.

So, basically, everything that human beings do causes harm to the environment. But does that mean that we stop using technology, or celebrating festivals or wearing fashionable clothes or stop eating at all? No, but we can always find ways to enjoy life in such a way that we do not harm the environment.

To start with, we can start celebrating our festivals in an eco-friendly way. Create idols with mud or clay, emphasize celebrating with lights instead of crackers, using organic materials like rice powder, dried flowers as rangoli powder instead of the traditional glass powder or artificial colours and recycling products like waste boxes and bottles to make interesting artifacts instead of buying new ones every year.

Usage of technology can't be reduced, but we can definitely try reducing e-waste by re-evaluating their usage, recycling them, donating or disposing of them in the safest ways.

As consumers of fashion, we can start analysing our needs for clothes and accessories. Paying more for long lasting clothes is always better than buying too many clothes at cheaper prices which can be retained for a shorter period of time. Upscale your old clothes and make something interesting out of them instead of throwing them out or rather passing it on to someone else. Learn to appreciate what you have and wear them till they are unwearable.

When it comes to food, we can't completely stop eating something that we love eating, but we can definitely stop consuming more than necessary. We tend to buy multiple things but end up wasting almost 25% of the food. Consume sustainable food like beans, organic vegetables, leafy vegetables, rice, lentils, organic fruits which are good for us as well as the environment.

Our small habits leave a big impact on the environment. Hence, we can't afford to say that if I do something wrong, it's okay because one person will not harm the environment much. We humans need to realise the sustainability that starts with us. No one will come to save our earth, if we don't start working towards saving it.

So, let's be responsible citizens, not only of the country, but the whole world and be the advocates for sustainability.

Sustainability- It starts with You

References:

- Author, G. (2013, November 26). *Why so much negligence towards Sustainable Environmental Practices?* Green Clean Guide. https://greencleanguide.com/why-so-much-negligence-towards-sustainable-environmental-practices/
- Brown, J. (n.d.). *The truth about processed foods' environmental impact.* BBC Future. https://www.bbc.com/future/article/20210617-the-truth-about-processed-foods-environmental-impact

- *Environmental Sustainability in the Fashion Industry.* (n.d.). https://www.genevaenvironmentnetwork.org/resources/updates/sustainable-fashion/
- *Here's the real impact of the food we eat on the environment.* (2020, February 6). World Economic Forum. https://www.weforum.org/agenda/2016/12/your-kitchen-and-the-planet-the-impact-of-our-food-on-the-environment
- James, M. (2022, May 4). *Most Sustainable Foods and How to Eat Sustainably.* TofuBud. https://tofubud.com/blogs/tips/most-sustainable-foods
- Shaikh, M. (2022, October 25). *After Diwali, air quality index in Mumbai hits moderate category | Details.* India Today. https://www.indiatoday.in/cities/mumbai/story/mumbai-news-air-quality-index-diwali-crackers-smoke-aqi-2289194-2022-10-25

II

Breathe Easy

Composed by - Dr. Reni Francis
Principal,
MES's Pillai College of Education and Research
Chembur, Mumbai.

> *As I went for my morning walk*
> *Time ticking on the clock*
> *Every breath that I took*
> *Was holding it like a nozzle on the hook.*
> *The speeding cars and motorbike*
> *Fuming the nature with a spike*
> *Walking on with a mask*
> *Not sure whom to ask*
> *When will the days be back*
> *To breathe easy without any hack*
> *Longing for a day*
> *That eases our way*
> *To a bright life ahead*
> *Always cheer spread*
> *This is the time to stand and act*
> *Otherwise, it will be late to react.*

Don't shut your ears and eyes today
Let's promise to be conscious everyday
Our actions create an impact
Let it be a strong part
Sustainable future is our aim
Let the tiny steps not go in vain.
Don't let these thoughts go breezy
Foster practices to breathe easy

Breathe Easy

III

Green Living- The Path Towards a Sustainable Future

Dr. Jaya Cherian

Assistant Professor,
MES's Pillai College of Education and Research
Chembur, Mumbai.

Today as human society is advances at a very rapid pace in all aspects at the same time we witness extreme climatic conditions, natural calamities and various other issues that is hazardous to us and the natural world around us. Safeguarding the environment is not simply a trendy thing to do but a necessity. As noted by Robert Swan, *'The greatest threat to our planet is the belief that someone else will save it.'* The responsibility of protecting our environment rests with each one of us.

Green living emerges from the principles of sustainable development. Sustainable development as defined by

UNESCO means development that meets the needs of the present without compromising the ability of future generations to meet their own needs. It implies that we live in such a way that we do not adversely impact the environment and leave the planet in peril for future generations. Green living is about living in a more environmentally conscious manner and ensure that we make such lifestyle choices that are beneficial or have minimal impact on the environment. Some of the green living practices that can set us on the path towards an eco-friendly way of life includes the following:

Energy efficient electrical devices

Household appliances consume a lot of energy and add to the emission of greenhouse gases thus causing damage to the environment. Energy efficient devices tend to use minimum amount of energy to complete their tasks. They reduce the exploitation of natural resources. Energy efficient appliances such as washing machines, refrigerators, air conditioners, dish washers etc. tend to emit less greenhouse gases reducing your carbon footprint and uses less water hence helps in water conservation. Use of electrical devices that are energy efficient will lead to less consumption of energy, reducing electricity bills leading to financial saving for the individual. We should also adopt habits such as unplugging electrical devices when they are not in use. There are many devices that we use which though we may switch off, there is still a slight flow of electricity. In order to save energy these devices need to be unplugged.

Home gardening

Another important way of adopting a greener living is by starting a home garden. In urban areas which is characterized by space constraints this may seem a difficult concept. But there are a variety of ideas that can be adopted to grow some green within your home premises. One can plant herbs, small plants, vegetables etc. in pots, windowsills as well as implement vertical gardening and terrace gardening. This also ensures that we have access to fresh and healthy vegetables. Home gardening is not just a way for a more sustainable living with a positive environmental impact, it also has positive impact on our health and wellbeing as we engage in the activities related to gardening. Developing our own green spaces helps in reducing our carbon footprint as well as reducing urban temperatures and provide a cooling environment for your home. The creation of these small green spaces can help in enabling cleaner air and reducing the impact of urban noises as plants are a natural sound barrier.

Recycling waste

Many of the materials that we discard as waste may end up in landfills and cause damage to the environment. It is necessary that we follow measures such as waste segregation. We can recycle and reuse many of the materials such as paper, plastic, metals etc. By following the appropriate processes of waste separation and recycling we can minimize the adverse impact of several materials that we use on the environment. We should avoid using single use plastics as they tend to be hazardous to animals who consume these plastics. These plastics take an extremely long time to decompose. Another important aspect of green living is that we should give a good thought to our consumption habits and the products that we buy. Today the consumption habits of people all over the world have increased manifold. Technological advancements have contributed to ease in trade and consumption across countries. We are consuming many times more than previous generations and consequently huge amounts of waste is also generated. We need to consider the impact of our consumption habits and the products that we use on the environment and try to invest in products that are more suitable for green living.

Planting trees

As human society makes immense progress in its development and growth it has led to a marked increase in deforestation leading to the planet losing large amount of its green cover. This is detrimental to the planet and to the health of human beings. Trees are a natural resource that sustain many forms of life. The carbon dioxide levels have been increasing at alarming levels. We tend to neglect the fact that, it is trees that take up carbon dioxide and release oxygen, essential for the survival of all. Many animal and bird species are endangered or facing extinction due to loss of their natural habitat. Tree roots go deep into the soil and act as anchors holding the soil, thus preventing soil erosion and reduce the impact of many natural calamities such as floods, landslides etc. Trees cleanse the air and cool the environment. To mitigate the adverse impact of deforestation we need to engage in and support tree plantation.

Rainwater harvesting

Water is an essential resource, and our use of this precious resource has increased to such a great extent that we are facing the threat of water scarcity. Though the planet is 75% covered with water only 2.7% of the total water is freshwater. The impact of climate change, rising population, increasing water pollution etc. scarcity of potable water will soon be a closer reality. By practicing rainwater harvesting we can utilize this for our daily needs and reduce the strain on the available water resources. It refers to collecting and storing rainwater for human use. The process of treating water and pumping to people's homes consumes a lot of energy. Rainwater harvesting is a more energy efficient process. It also reduces water bills and hence has financial benefits to the user. The greater number of people adopt this practice the less strain on the natural water supplies as well as the city's water supplies leading to conservation of water resource.

Adopting a green living lifestyle is not only about benefiting the environment, which is the need of the hour, but we need to understand that in the process we are removing materials that are toxic to our health from our lives and thus ensuring a cleaner, healthier life for ourselves. We need to adopt such eco-friendly behaviors that is based on the foundation of 'respect for nature' and leave a safe planet for our future generations to live in.

Green Living- The Path Towards a Sustainable Future

References:

- https://www.greenjournal.co.uk/2019/08/
- https://www.yonature.com/green-living-10-best-ways-live-green-life
- https://biofriendlyplanet.com/nature/environment/50-ways-to-make-your-life-more-environmentally-friendly/
- https://www.greenly.earth/blog-en/what-is-green-living
- https://www.conserve-energy-future.com/15-ideas-for-sustainable-living.php

IV
Way towards the Greener Living

Mr. Rajendra B. Deshmukh

Assistant Professor,
MES's Pillai College of Education and Research
Chembur, Mumbai.

Environmental pollution is a must unit in the school curricula of all the grades and in all the educational boards. It includes the causes, effects and the control measures of pollution. Assessment questions on the pollution unit are mostly open-ended questions where the students write anything and as per the directions of the moderators even for the board exams the teachers are advised to award the full marks. In response to the question what steps you can take to control the pollution and make environment a better place, students mostly come up with textbook answers like framing strict laws, controlling deforestation etc. i.e., most of the answers are derived from the textbooks.

If pollution control and protection of the environment has to occur each one of us needs to contribute. The change makers (teachers) through the future change makers (students) as an effect or change of behavior due to the classroom learning should take the onus of contributing to the greener living. Closing the taps when not required, switching off lights and fans while leaving the classroom, using things optimally and avoiding wastage, travelling together to decrease expenses and pollution, using public transport whenever possible, not harming the plants and animals and avoiding throwing clothes, utensils, bags and gadgets just because they are old should become habits.

Not using things even if they are in a better condition and usable, just for a change, is contributing to the environmental degradation. If the students understand the effect of our day-to-day wrong habits and actions, they will ensure ecofriendly behavior.

In the words of the Mahatma Gandhi, if we could change ourselves, the world would also change. Students when understand the importance of the available resources they will go for the economical and judicious usage of them. They will practice the '5R' Mantra i.e., refuse, reduce, reuse, repurpose, and then recycle, take steps to reduce the impact of consumerism on the climate change, stay away from the fast fashion and single use plastic, start focusing on sustainable solutions and the Circular Economy.

The teaching community if starts looking at the students as the instruments of change of the society and motivate, prepare them for the desired change ardently, the change is inevitable. It is the time teachers leave behind the theoretical lecture method and pave the way for the empirical and multi-sensory learning.

The teacher if demonstrates to the students how a leakage in a tap result in wastage of litres of water, how manufacturing units creates different types of pollution, how things can be disposed, decomposed, reused and recycled, how less consumption of things leads to less pollution, what is environment friendly and what is not and how fuels, electricity, water and other resources can be conserved they will get an opportunity to practice the sustainable practices.

Arranging the field visits to the places engaged in research and execution of sustainable practices, interacting with the people engaged in the protection of the environment and the experts from the allied fields, attending environmental summits, organizing inspiring talks and undertaking research projects related to the natural resources and the environment will provide the students the required push to do something worth with regard to the environmental protection.

Valuing Sustainable Development Goals (SDGs) adopted by the UNESCO in the educational institutes, undertaking initiatives, planning, executing and implementing programs for the successful achievement of them should be also one of the priorities of the educational institutes. Trained and motivated school leaders will ensure the implementation of the practices leading towards achievement of SDGs at the micro level.

The rate at which environmental degradation is happening quick steps needs to be taken and needs to continue in an uninterrupted nature in the future. The participation of young learners in the protection of environment is thus important. When the students visit the places in their surrounding as part of their educational visits understand various types of environmental degradation activities and see their impact on the surrounding, they come across with the severity of the issues. The research projects given to link the classroom learning with the actual practices in the field inspire students to do something special for the environment protection. There is need to move towards taking action for greener living instead of just talk on the various issues. Halfhearted efforts are not going to help us know there is need for aimed, goal oriented, planned, dedicated and sustained efforts from everyone. It cannot be a government or NGO or few individuals endeavor alone.

Way towards the Greener Living

V
Live Green, Live Well!

Ms. Diandra Pinto

Assistant Professor,
MES's Pillai College of Education and Research
Chembur, Mumbai.

While 'greener living' majorly implies sustainable practices for the health of our planet, this chapter seeks to explore how sustainable practices and the mere act of getting out into nature is just as important for our health as human beings.

According to the World Health Organization, more than 450 million people worldwide suffer from a mental disorder, and this number is increasing. People living in urban areas are at a higher risk of developing anxiety and mental health problems. The age-old doctor's remedy of 'a change of scenery' is, in practice, a very effective one. Being in nature can have a positive effect on our health for several different reasons.

Our human bodies, and more specifically our brains have several chemicals that are interdependent on each other and regulate our behaviour and moods. Being out in nature is known to boost serotonin, the happiness hormone in our body. This leads not only to a more positive disposition but also an increase in activity in the parts of the brain that are associated with emotional stability. Several outdoor activities are known to reduce the stress hormone cortisol in our bodies.

Walking in nature has direct benefits on our physical and mental health. Apart from the usual physical benefits, nature walks boost brain performance, reduces stress and reduces the risk of heart diseases. It also increases our exposure to natural sunlight which is important to maintain healthy levels of vitamin D. The combination of fresh air and exercise leads to improved mood and self-esteem. Hiking up hills or mountains have the added benefit of making you more mindful. Climbing uphill increases the intensity of the exercise compared to a regular nature walk while descending down a hill or mountain forces us to be mindful as we need to focus on each step to descend safely. Latest research has found that nature walks also have positive implications for attention, memory and also creative problem solving. Being out in nature is relaxing and exposes us to several other activities that force us to be more mindful that improves our overall wellbeing and can reduce levels of stress and anxiety.

Birdwatching is an excellent example of a mindfulness activity while outdoors. It makes us focus our attention on something, in this case, the bird we are trying to spot or observe and takes our mind off whatever may be troubling us. Our senses, sight and hearing are tuned into the moment. Stillness is also an important aspect while birding so we do not inadvertently drive the birds away. Birding connects us with beauty and joy which in turn has a positive impact on our wellbeing. The colours, shapes, sounds/calls, flight patterns are some of the things that we would pay attention to while birding. One has to be very present while bird watching and this clears our minds from anxiety and other stressors.

People enjoy spending time near waterfalls, fountains, and water gushing on rocks near rivers or the beach. The reason is more than just the sound of the gushing water and its visual appeal. Being around gushing water tends to have a positive effect on our health. This is because of the negative oxygen ions generated by the crashing water. The negative ions refer to oxygen atoms that have picked up an extra electron, thus the negative charge. According to Pierce J. Howard, the negative ions increase the flow of oxygen to the brain which can increase alertness and energy.

Adopting a more sustainable lifestyle gives us a sense of purpose that can be very rewarding. This most often leads to a more minimalist lifestyle that forces us to be more mindful about the way we go about our lives; whether it is the products we use, the food we consume or waste. Adopting a greener lifestyle has tremendous benefits not just for the planet, but also our socio-emotional wellbeing. Making an effort to adopt a more sustainable lifestyle and get back to nature impacts the way we think and subsequently our mental and physical health as well.

While being outdoors has several benefits of our physical and mental health, practicing sustainability also has cognitive benefits in addition to reducing our carbon footprint. Sustainable living and spending time in nature contributes to a happier, healthier and stress-free life.

Live Green, Live Well!

VI

The Proverbial 3Rs

Dr. Spoty Karthik

Assistant Professor,
Rizvi College of Education
Khar, Mumbai.

During my young days we never heard the slogan of 'reduce, reuse and recycling' but our homes were always doing it. Plastic containers were not seen, plastic bags were very rare. My mother stored the groceries in glass and tin containers always washed, dried and refilled them. Harvested grains and finished rice were stored in big wooden granary called *'pathayam'* which is heirloom passed on to generations. Our maid used to carry a bamboo basket when going to market and for grocery shopping. The fish monger used to carry the fish in a matted basket made from coconut leaves. Ash which generated from burning of firewood was used as detergent for utensil cleaner as well as a nutrient for plants. The sacred ash was used as vermillion on the forehead drawn as bands. Clothes were never thrown away until it is completely worn out. It gets handed over from us to siblings/cousins, to workers and finally to cleaning cloth. I remember my mother's silk sari being worn by our house help as her wedding sari. Of course, the slogan of 3Rs originated later as a government initiative to promote environmental friendly practices when household thrash increased tremendously.

In fact, we confuse the idea of 3Rs as something we learnt from the west but sometimes, we need to learn to look inwards, when it prevailed here for generations for however long our civilization is. There are many a thing which all kids of the 70's to 90's would probably relate to. We pass our text books to our siblings, cousins or neighbours. Text book was considered sacred and representation of *Devi Saraswati* and so it was never thrown to the dust bin. Unused pages of notebooks were sewn together to make a rough book. We used our pencils to the tiniest bit till our small hand could no longer hold it. The ink refill pens were treasured since there were no cheap 'use and throw' alternatives available. Affordability was not just the reason why we reused and recycled but it was because we valued things.

In today's times of consumerism solid waste generated in urban areas has accumulated tremendously that its management is a humungous task. Traditional way of burning is no more adopted realising the harmful toxic chemicals like dioxins, furans and oxides of carbon, nitrogen and sulphur emitted during burning. Dumping yards creates leachates which have carcinogens. Mindless generation of waste resultant of the rampant 'use and throw' culture needs to be dealt with sustainable practices. The first step towards it should start from the very word waste itself, revisiting it by asking the question 'whether what we call waste is really waste?' And the way forward can be best put through the words of professor Paul Connet (even though it sounds utopian), *'if we can't reuse it, recycle it or compost, industry shouldn't be making it.*

The present scenario clearly emphasises the proverbial 3Rs adding a fourth R – 'Refuse' to limit our consumption.

The Proverbial 3Rs

VII

Eco-Friendly Home

Ms. Athira S. R.

Alumni, Batch 2020-2022
MES's Pillai College of Education and Research
Chembur, Mumbai.

The world is progressively shifting towards sustainable modes of living. With growing environmental awareness and the need to reduce carbon footprint, more people have started embracing sustainable practices in their lives. Right from making changes in lifestyles to designing better homes that reflect their values. Cultivating a green home is not easy, but once you have Committed, you will reap many rewards—including Significant financial savings as well as the hard-won Feeling that you are doing your part to secure a Sustainable future for your family and your planet. So, an eco-friendly home is an environment friendly home that optimizes its impact on the environment. These homes are energy-efficient and they do offer a way forward in architecture and construction amidst the increasing intensity of climate change.

Living an eco-friendly lifestyle goes beyond buying eco-friendly products. It entails living a green lifestyle and a green future is possible with an environment –friendly approach by way of sustainable home design.

Here, I introduce to you my sustainable eco-friendly home which has been designed to keep the carbon footprints to a minimum amount and maximum use of recyclable products.

Firstly, I would Like to talk about the selection of the site for my home. I have made sure there is availability of public transport in the locality of my home. Also, while designing the roof of my home, I have made sure it's out of shade in order to facilitate the later usage of solar panels.

You can see I have chosen a place with ample shaded trees which helped me cut back on heating and cooling costs easily. Also, I made sure to choose a place with garden space as well to offer many possibilities.

Secondly, I have focused my attention on monitoring the amount of water consumed by installing water meters and rain water harvesting. This way I can optimize the amount of water wasted otherwise cheaply. And whatever wastewater is generated is again reused for non-potable uses like flushing and landscaping. You can see in my bathroom that I have made low consumption faucets and shower-heads to conserve water thus ensuring maximum utilization and minimum wastage.

Most importantly I have used the cleanest source of electricity by installing solar panels on my roof top which is getting the optimum amount of sunlight. I have also taken care of roofing material with High solar reflectance and thermal emittance so as to Minimize heat island effect and maximize energy Savings.

One thing u must have observed is that I have used LED bulbs wherever I can instead of traditional incandescent bulbs because we all know Led bulbs consume minimal energy

Ensuring an efficient municipal solid waste management system was a high priority requirement for me because otherwise it can create serious negative environmental impact including infectious diseases, land and water pollution, blockage of drainages, and loss of biodiversity. Hence, as a sustainable occupant, I have made sure to segregate our wastes at sources before they are taken to landfills.

I have also ensured all products I use have minimal packaging as u can see. There is no waste in my home as my policy is to keep only what you need in your home. I often donate any Items that are in usable condition to orphanages, Community homes or other institutions that could putt them to better use.

Apart from these I have been using reusable water bottles, reusable cutlery in my kitchen as u can see. I do use rags and clothes for cleaning.

Now coming to the aesthetic point of view I have been using articles made from jute like bags, wall hangings, ropes, other than using the ones made from plastic or leatherette. You can see me using organic cotton items like curtains, rugs, bedsheets, upholstery etc.

I have stuck to using mosaics which use scraps of marble, quartz, granite or recycled glass chips, poured with a Cement binder to form a composite material for better aesthetic looks and is one of the most environmentally friendly material options for floors.

Lastly, I have Grown indoor plants which act as natural air filters and reduce carbon footprints. I have also invested in setting up a small kitchen farm so as to ensure more greenery.

All in all, the focus has been given to utilizing the maximum available daylight efficiently.

I hope this inspires you to live kinder to the environment.

Our environment is going through significant changes, many of them not for the better. There are many reasons behind this transition, such as pollution, greenhouse effect, deforestation and various others. These problems are slowly depleting the planet that we live on in different ways, and severely impacting our health as well. To combat this, there is a dire need of adopting an eco-friendly lifestyle as our lives are exposed to a lot of risks. Plus, it is high time we do our bit in saving the environment. So, investing in an eco-friendly house is going to provide you with long-term health benefits, and make a better tomorrow for future generations to come.

Eco-Friendly Home

VIII
Healthy Change in Lifestyle!

Ms. Aishwarya Laxmi Nadar
S. Y. B. Ed. Student, Batch 2021-2023
MES's Pillai College of Education and Research
Chembur, Mumbai.

> ***"Cutting waste food is a delicious way of saving money,***
> ***helping to feed the world and protect the planet."***
> ***- Tristram Stuart***

The most undemanding and eco-friendly process is to recycle our food waste. The wasting of food is costly to consumers, which depletes the natural resources and it degrades the environment. Food waste contributes to landfills and produces more amount of methane and harmful gases. Leftover food items in our home can be used as recycled food products for the next day's breakfast or lunch. These food items can also be refrigerated or frozen and can be consumed later. Recycling waste food can reduce the amount of waste pollution and make the environment more fit to survive.

Food wastes can be recycled in many ways such as through DIY beauty products. For example, the leftover lemon can be rubbed inside the fingernails and the acid from the juice brightens the nails after washing the nails with warm water. The coffee grounds or sugar can be used as a natural exfoliant if applied once a week to the face. Using banana peels to polish the leaves of plants at home or using them to rub on leather shoes, by avoiding the chemicals, will make them look as good as new. Polishing the expensive silverware with banana peel will make them sparkle. Also, this peel is used as a teeth whitener. We can soak the banana peel overnight in water and use that water to water the plants the next day, this provides the plants with more nutritious products, which contain rich potassium and phosphorus.

Food wastes can also be used as an aroma for a home environment. For example, the citrus peels placed down the garbage disposal, will get rid of the disposal smell. Boiling these peels in little water will create a natural home air freshener. Food wastes can be made as infusions like zests or peels of lemons, oranges, limes, grapefruit or tangerines are perfect ingredients to infuse many foods into olive oil or water and can be created into a more flavourful recipe.

The leftover foods can be used to reinvent fried rice, soups, and hash. The seeds and cutting of lettuce, ginger, celery, green onions, avocado, and many other veggies can be regrown by planting them into the soil with adequate water and providing them with plenty of sunlight, which will give us more veggies for the price of one!

The food which is wasted can be collected and made into other yummy dishes. The leftover bread can be cut and baked into small crusts to make them into croutons, which can be used on top of the casserole for salads and soups. The end of the bread should not be thrown out. It can be edible by using a trick, i.e., by adding the brown bread into the sugar container. This will soften the bread and prevent it from turning solid.

The apple peels, the core of an apple, apricot peels, and strawberry tops with a few other ingredients can be infused and made into jam, giving a natural fruity taste. The leftover carrot peels, celery tops, or potato skins can be combined into a broth or liquid to make a flavoured soup or stock. These food scraps can also be used as a natural fertilizer, which enriches the soil for the plants to grow. Eggs and nut shells like peanuts and pistachios can be used as a natural fertilizer for plants. The leaves, peels and seeds of food waste is also recycled and used as an ornament made by resin.

The discarded parts of vegetables and fruits such as peels, pulp, and leaves are often very rich in bioactive phytochemicals. These bioactive phytochemicals are the chemical compounds that are produced by plants. These extracts can be used in pharmaceuticals, food preservatives, and dietary supplements, which would help in preventing more wastage of food. Nowadays, the technological innovations and advancements in science and research will further optimize the performance of the products which is wasted.

At present, the burning of waste products in India has a low calorific value ranging from 1,411 kcal/kg to 2,150 kcal/kg. The food waste is an environmental, economic and ethical problem, which leads to not only the loss of caloric intake but also it leads to the destruction of needless to the finite resources.

By reducing food wastage, a noticeable change can be brought in the economy of many countries and it can increase the standard of living of the people.

References:

- https://earth.org/quotes-about-food
- https://swachhindia.ndtv.com/garbage-management-crisis
- https://www.digitaljournal.com/pr/organic-waste-recycling-
- https://healthcenter.uga.edu/10-things-you-can-do-with-food-scraps-to-reduce-food-waste/
- https://www.dcw.co.uk/the-importance-of-food-waste-recycling/
- https://www.hennepin.us/choose-to-reuse/tips/leftover-ideas
- https://www.conserve-energy-future.com/smart-ways-recycle-food
- https://www.science.org.au/curious/earth-environment/transforming-food-waste-making-something-out-rubbish
- https://www.ipl.org/essay/Food-Wastage-Essay-FJJJMYBQAQU
- https://nap.nationalacademies.org/read/25876/chapter/2
- http://www.inquiriesjournal.com/articles/890/3/the-consequences-of-food-waste

Healthy Change in Lifestyle!

IX

Zero Waste Cooking: The Future of Food Waste Management and Recycling

Ms. Janhavi Yadav

S. Y. B. Ed. Student, Batch 2021-2023
MES's Pillai College of Education and Research
Chembur, Mumbai.

India and its ever-increasing population are faced with a paradoxical problem of having a severe food shortage in the country and on the other hand the nation also has serious issues when it comes to management and recycling of its food waste. The amount of food wasted in India is almost equal to the amount of food consumed by the whole of UK, the disparity in the populations of both the nations can be blamed for this to a certain extent.

India is a land of festivals and over the top celebrations and we pride ourselves on this and rightly so. But occasions like weddings, family functions, communal feasts etc. Contribute greatly to the food wastage happening in the country.

What's the reason behind food wastage in our country?

In India we believe in huge celebrations, massive feasts, but the larger the wedding, or the celebrations the more in the food waste that comes from them. The restaurants and hotels also contribute greatly to the food waste in the country. The amount of food waste in India has increased enormously in the last 5 years. Although, a few restaurants in India do use food controllers to avoid food spoilage and donate or give away the food that is not served to the guests, these measures do not help the situation on a large scale.

What can we do?

Greater changes can be brought about in our society and our country at large only if we are willing to execute them on the grass root or individual level. In order to tackle the problem of food waste management in our country, we need to start small and bring about changes in our own choices and life style as a whole. Only if we try our best to change the food waste scenario on a personal level, we can expect positive results and better management and recycling of food waste to be reflected on a larger scale. **Zero waste cooking** is one of the most popular, sustainable and eco-friendly ways of food waste management and recycling.

What is Zero Waste Cooking?

Zero waste cooking simply refers to leaving no waste or scraps in your meal preps. While following the method of zero waste cooking one makes sure that he/she uses all the parts or the whole of the ingredient in the preparation of the meal without leaving any waste behind. For example: While using vegetables, the peeled veg is used in the preparation of the meal, while the peels of the vegetables are either used for preparing a vegetable stock or for making a compost. No part of the ingredient is thrown away without recycling it first.

The zero-waste method is not just limited to the kitchen one can follow this method in every single aspect of their life however, in order to successfully follow a zero-waste lifestyle one has to plan, organize, strategize and make preparations in advance

Zero waste is based on the classic principles of **Reduce, Reuse** and **Recycle**:

- **Reduce**: Use only the quantity of ingredients you actually need. Cook in adequate portions make sure that the quantity of leftovers is as small as possible, as they usually end up making the trip to the bin in a day or two since cooked food ends up spoiling easily.
- **Reuse**: Make it a point to reuse the containers that the ingredients and the cooked food items like rice dishes, curries are packed in, instead of throwing them away right after they are emptied of their contents.
- **Recycle**: The food scraps like peels, seeds etc. can be easily recycled by composting them within your houses, if you have the access to adequate equipment and the space to do the same. If it is something that seems beyond your means you can also donate your wet waste and food scraps to organizations that can compost them

for you.

Here's why you should start the zero-waste cooking method right now:

- Can be practice and implemented in one's life easily. You can try making your next meal with zero waste.
- Its cost efficient, if you buy less, recycle and reuse more you end up spending a lot less than you would otherwise.
- You can do your bit in order to improve the health of our environment right now.
- By not wasting food you're indirectly putting some food on a needy person's plate.
- It is one of the most important and impactful ways of dealing with the food wastage in our country.
- It is the future of food waste management and recycling.

XI

Greener Living is the New Lifestyle !

Ms. Phatak Siddhi Suvarnakumar

S. Y. B. Ed. Student, Batch 2021-2023
MES's Pillai College of Education and Research
Chembur, Mumbai.

The word lifestyle means the way in which a person lives. In this era of competition, humans are running behind wealth creation in spite of knowing that real wealth is good health and being able to experience life to its fullest. Good health comes from good lifestyle. Whether it is the individual human body or the larger cosmic body, essentially, they are made of five elements or the pancha bhutas – earth, water, fire, air and akasha. All these are elements of nature as well. Hence, we need to use them cautiously and preserve them for future generation as existence of humans depends on the existence of these five elements that we get from nature. Greener living is the best way to take care of the nature we live in.

"Green living" means making sustainable choices about what we eat, how we travel, what we buy, and how we use and dispose of it. In short, we need to think about the choices that we make, how our choices will have impact on our nature/ environment as it will directly or indirectly affect us in the near future. Our choices have impact on every element of the nature. For instance, if one family member is ill then all other family members are disturbed in some not the other way, their schedule, work, health, sleeping patten, food, etc. everything is impacted. Similarly, the way in which human beings live, our choices, etc. everything has impact on the nature and environment we say in. this is because we are a part of this ecosystem (family).

We should be aware of what we eat as it not only has impact on our health and mind but also on our planet. We do not give a second thought to how our food ends up on our plates, but making a few simple shifts in the way we purchase food can have a big impact on the food system and, by extension, the environment.

- Green eating means choosing a predominantly plant-based diet.
- Green eating means choosing responsibly-grown fruits and vegetables.
- Green eating mean eating with the seasons and supporting local food systems.
- Green eating means reducing food and kitchen waste.
- Green eating means not wasting the food.
- Finally, green eating means sharing and celebrating food.

It is essential that we implement 3 R's- Reduce, Reuse, Recycle to save the environment and move our lifestyle to greener living. The first R in the waste hierarchy is "Reduce."

Reduce

Use of cloth napkins instead of using paper tissues (cloth napkins can be reused after wash, but paper napkins will only increase the amount of waste)

"Wastage of paper while printing." You should print on both sides of a paper.

You can switch to electronic mails instead of sending letters via papers.

"Use & throw type of products" should be avoided as these products do not run for a long time (Choose the products with a long life)

Disposables like plates, cups, spoon, etc. are used to minimize the workload, but unfortunately, this leads to a considerable amount of waste accumulations.

Reuse

The old tires can be best used as a swing, which is one of the favourite time-pass for kids.

Use old newspapers to pack old items to store. Use newspapers to wrap things when you are moving from one place to another.

You can donate your old books & notebooks to poor kids so that they can also study to fulfil their dreams.

Your old clothes which are not in use now and you are planning to dump them; you can donate these clothes to needy people.

Recycle

You can also buy those items from the market which are made up of recycled material.

Try to buy an eco-friendly product from the market that is composed of recyclable material. The leftover material can be easily recycled after its usage.

Try to choose non-toxic material or products so that it can be recycled without any hazardous effects.

You can also invent different ways from your end to recycling various items and products.

Its rightly said that we should reuse the past, recycle the present, save the future because better environment means better tomorrow. Choices that we make today decides our future. Hence, our lifestyle decides our survival. Go green, that's what I mean!

References:

- Green living - Appropedia: The sustainability wiki
- What are the Five Elements or Pancha Bhutas? (sadhguru.org) https://isha.sadhguru.org/us/en/wisdom/article/five-elements-pancha-bhuta
- Definition Of Green Living - Green Home Adviser
- What is Green Eating? Your Sustainable Eating Start Guide (forkintheroad.co)
- https://www.earthreminder.com/3rs-of-environment-reduce-reuse

Greener Living is the New Lifestyle !

XII

Change your Transportation Choices, to see how the Environment Rejoices.

Ms. Riddhi Maru

S. Y. B. Ed. Student, Batch 2021-2023
MES's Pillai College of Education and Research
Chembur, Mumbai.

"Everyone wants to Get Back to Nature, But no one on The Foot."
-Werner Mitsch

The recent trends of road trips, sedentary lifestyle and lousiness, post pandemic safety, rapid development in urban India and many other reasons have resulted in a tremendous increase in the number of motor vehicles. In the last decade, the sales of motor vehicles have doubled in some areas of India. Rapid urbanization and growth of motor vehicles impose a serious effect on human life and environment. And a prime example of this was seen during the covid-19 lockdown. Restricted human interaction with nature during this crisis time appeared as a blessing for nature and environment. Reports from all over the world indicated that after the outbreak of COVID-19, environmental conditions including air quality and water quality in rivers improved and wildlife was blooming. Vehicles and transport sector individually contribute around 90% of total emissions and majorly leads to air pollution. Air pollution is a serious environmental health threat to humans. Injurious health effects range from headache, nausea, difficulty in breathing, skin irritations, birth defects and cancer etc.

In this context, Sustainable transport arises. Sustainable transport reduces the adverse impact associated with this increased urban mobility and in promoting more environment – friendly modes of transport. The sustainable transport definition can be best described as any type of transport that does not rely on the world's natural resources to power it. The goal of sustainable transport is to reduce adverse impacts on the environment. It includes both private transport modes and public transport modes.

Some benefits even extend far beyond solving road transport issues. Several benefits of sustainable transportation are:

- Reduces Environmental Footprint
- Creates Less Congestion
- Saves Money

- Creates Jobs
- Improves Health

One big factor which encourages private modes of transport is the high density of population in India. It is very difficult to manage the population of 1.39 billion. Due to the high density of population, there is a lack of proper parking spaces, no proper footpaths available for pedestrians and even if there are properly marked footpaths some vendors and shops might use that area for themselves. Even if we take an example of train at peak hours the rush is so bad that sometimes it is impossible to even stand properly. Even in context of buses, if the buses are full at peak hours, they don't even wait at bus stops. All this wastage of time, over crowd in trains and buses, encourages people to use private modes of transport.

By keeping all this in mind, many steps have been taken in last few years. Though the implementation and planning for such a populated country may take time to build such a modern and sustainable infrastructure. But here are some examples of future - thinking cities taking concrete steps towards sustainable transport, what they are doing, and what you can learn from them.

Pune

Pune has an estimated population of 3.99 million, is a rapidly developing city with a growing, robust economy, and fortunately, an ambitious plan to improve mobility. In 2015, the city launched the Rainbow Bus Rapid Transit (BRT) system. Today, the corridor route is of 39 kilometres, serving 120,000 people per day. Rainbow BRT has high-quality and best-practice design features, and has brought more than 12 percent of its ridership from other modes, primarily private cars. Rainbow BRT, one of the first BRTs in India, has added 200 CNG and 25 electric buses to its fleet. It plans to add 400 CNG and 125 electric buses in the upcoming year to grow the fleet to 2500 buses by. The BRT corridor has expanded to 50 kilometres and plans to expand the corridor to 90 kilometres by end of year. Pune has become a regional leader in complete streets, in which streets are designed for all users, rather than only for cars; pedestrians, cyclists, motorists, and transit riders are given safe access with the complete streets approach.

Pune's successes have already inspired many cities in India to adopt new measures for sustainability and equity. Nashik has hired urban design firms for its Complete Streets network; Chennai is keen on expanding its complete streets into a network and setting up a BRT system, learning from Pune's journey so far.

Ahmedabad

Ahmedabad has a population of more than 6.3 million and an extended population of 7.2 million. It is the sixth largest city and seventh largest metropolitan area of India. The bus rapid transport system was created to serve a growing population. It aims to enable the higher adoption of public transport by reducing the stop time of the buses at the intersections and improving their travel time. Passenger numbers have also grown, from 18,000 at the start to nearly 130,000 today. The route has grown from 12 kilometres to 45 kilometres and growing. Furthermore, Janmarg has planned and designed the system including a street only for pedestrians and for walking.

From these examples, it's evident that solutions to sustainable transportation already exist. Some current sustainable transportation solutions that can be implemented include:

- Extra road spaces for pedestrians and bikers must be developed.
- To discourage the use of cars in populated areas, high toll rates can be implied.
- Encouraging non-motorized modes of transport like walking, cycling, and scooters with dedicated lanes, while discouraging the frequent use of private motorized transport.
- Planning and designing new transit routes that are more sustainable and upgrading old ones.
- Ensuring effective implementation and coordination of sustainable mobility modes.
- Unnecessary idling of cars, trucks, and school buses pollutes the air, wastes fuel, and causes excess engine wear.
- When getting home deliveries or shopping online, consider asking to have all your packages sent in one shipment and with minimal packaging. For scheduled home deliveries, try to be flexible by choosing longer time windows so delivery trucks can optimize their routes and avoid extra trips.
- Walk or bike when you can, take public transit (trains, buses) when possible, carpool with friends instead of driving alone, and work from home periodically if your job allows it.
- When shopping for a new car, look for fuel efficient vehicles with low greenhouse gas emissions. These cars can help the environment while potentially saving you money on fuel costs at the pump.

BUY LESS, CHOOSE WELL, AND MAKE IT LAST.

- A review of vehicular pollution in urban India and its effects on human health by Chetana Khandar and Sharda Kosankar.
- https://climate.selectra.com/en/advice/sustainable-transport
- https://www.epa.gov/transportation-air-pollution-and-climate-change/
- what-you-can-do-reduce-pollution-vehicles-and
- https://www.itdp.org/2019/06/27/pune-india-wins-2020-sustainable-transport-award/
- https://cop23.unfccc.int/climate-action/momentum-for-change/lighthouse-activities/
- the-ahmedabad-bus-rapid-transit-system-in-india

Change your Transportation Choices, to see how the Environment Rejoices.

XIII

Sustainable Lifestyle and its Importance

Ms. Santhana Preetha Shanmugavel
S. Y. B. Ed. Student, Batch 2021-2023
MES's Pillai College of Education and Research
Chembur, Mumbai.

Sustainable living involves decreasing the quantity of resources available from earth that we use to help protect it. Sustainable living is also known as "Earth Harmony Living", or "net zero living". "The best way to predict the future is to create it"- By Peter Drucker. There are numerous methods that can be undertaken in order to protect natural resources such as reducing the use of energy, shifting to use eco-friendly products and changing diet. In short, to live a sustainable lifestyle we should try to have as little of an impact on the earth as far as possible, while also trying to replace the resources we use. If each one of us gets adapt a green lifestyle, then probably we would not be facing dangerous issues like Global Warming or deforestation. Each one would be doing their part in order to protect the environment. Many people pollute the environment knowingly or unknowingly that there is no planet. Accepting a green lifestyle controls the people around us to think twice about protecting or safeguarding the environment. Children who are environmentally conscious must be encouraged more to protect the natural resources because they are the future generation and they must know and be aware of the importance of protecting the natural resources. It is simple enough to understand that buying renewable containers guarantees that pollution is remarkably reduced. Going paperless is another good example to lessen these issues. There are several ways in which we can reduce the usage of paper, few of them are, prefer to receive digital letters and notices, ask shopkeepers or any kind of suppliers to mail you a receipt instead of printing you a receipt. Aquatic animals are majorly facing issues due to too much plastic inside the ocean. By introducing some small changes to our lifestyle, we can minimize carbon footprints which are not good for our environment which in turn can help to tackle these life-threatening issues.

Acquiring a green lifestyle is also good for our health since it is always wise to protect foods that are chemical free.

Some of the major advantage of changing our lifestyle into sustainable living are encapsulated below:

1. **Dewearing Environmental Pollution :**

The crystal-clear advantage of going sustainable is that it helps to lessen environmental pollution. We should cut of use of plastic within our household and acquire more sustainable method of keeping food. Plastic is considered to be the chief pollutant in environment and it causes too much damage as it is.

1. **Cost of Energy can be diminished :**

Utilization of solar energy instead of using electricity is considered to be the best option and this can ultimately save our electricity bills.

3. **Protect Natural Resources :**

Going green also means protecting the resources that our available to us. We can begin by setting up a habit for planting trees. We must make sure in order to involve our entire family so that our young generation can build up with these values implanted within them. Apart from solar energy we can also make use of water from Stream to inundate our garden. It is very important to take up gardening, so that our family members can consume clean food. Farming is also best way of managing stress and lead healthy lifestyle.

4. **Its Economical :**

Green Lifestyle are notably cheaper in the market. With today's growing economy we can opt for cheaper products for better living. Going Green means conducting a healthier life because our diet will significantly consist of fruits as well as vegetables. These food consists all the nutrients that are required for us to live longer.

5. **Impact change in your community :**

All it takes one person to impact a better change in the community. When other people in our community look how the way you are leading a healthier life, then automatically they will try to follow the same lifestyle. This in turn will bring change within our community. Acquiring a Green Lifestyle will help in maintaining a clean environment. If you show other people about considering the environment, they will gradually learn the same.

Going Green is the best way of contributing to environmental conservation. It is more important than ever to adopt a green lifestyle. These small changes can help reduce the pollution that threatens our health and our environment, while also protecting our natural resources. This lifestyle also makes sure that we lead a Healthier Lifestyle. When we all try to take small steps towards protecting our earth's natural resources, we all can bring in greater rewards.

References:

- https://www.wessexwater.co.uk/community/blog/14-ways-to-live-a-more-sustainable-lifestyle

Sustainable Lifestyle and its Importance

XIV

Approach towards a Greener & Sustainable Lifestyle

Ms. Sayed Mahvash Athar

S. Y. B. Ed. Student, Batch 2021-2023
MES's Pillai College of Education and Research
Chembur, Mumbai.

To live a better quality life is to live a life in an environment which is toxic free, clean & healthy for all – humans, plants and animals. To obtain such an environment, it is quite necessary for humans to adopt a lifestyle which is "greener" & more "sustainable."

To obtain a greener lifestyle is to minimize practices which will cause harm to the environment as well as take into consideration the health of the planet & its animals. In simple terms, living a greener & sustainable lifestyle means making choices that will conserve the environment. These choices are eco-friendly & thus, ethically right. The main question that arises though is how to go green & live sustainably.

The ways in which an individual can change their lifestyle to a more sustainable one is actually endless. These ways or to be more specific – these choices are both; expensive as well as inexpensive. But the impact these choices leave on our planet & us is incredible.

Greener, healthier & sustainable lifestyle choices:

Throwing food which you no longer need not only affects the environment but also is one of the major contributors of wasting the natural resources. To stop this from happening one needs to buy items in proper amount. Also, if the food is not needed anymore stray animals will be more than happy to consume it. Instead of throwing items like chapatti, rice, biscuits, etc. look around your area or simply keep bits of food near your house. If no stray animals will consume it, a flying crow sure will. This way food is not wasted, environment is protected & it fills the empty stomach of animals & birds.

Annually, 400 million tonnes of plastic waste is generated in the world. This not only affects the animals on land but also is harmful for the marine life. Thus, it is important to avoid using anything which is made from plastic. There are many alternatives such as bags made of cloth, straws made out of paper, products made from bamboo, etc. With this, preserving the marine life becomes easier since most of the times it is the marine life that diminishes because of plastic E.g. Turtles dying because of plastic straws.

Grow your own food – Not only will this benefit you but also will have a huge positive impact on the environment.

Since commercial farming pollutes the soil & water with its harmful chemicals, by growing your own food; you help reduce the soil & water pollution. Also, the amount of miles these foods travel before being consumed is high. Because of this, a threatening amount of carbon emission is emitted. By opting to grow your own food you help reduce carbon emissions, waste from food packaging materials, etc.

Another important thing to include in your lifestyle is to wear sustainable clothing & not hoarding what you don't need. Hoarding is harmful because for making products such as clothes many natural resources are used. Not to forget the amount of packaging in which the clothes come in. To reduce hoarding; donate whatever you don't need to orphanages, people in need or simply give it away to someone who will make use of it. This way the waste is less on the planet.

Save electricity & water – as simple & basic as it sounds, saving these two resources makes a huge difference. There are still many electricity generations which require burning of fossil fuels to produce energy. This leads to the shortage of fossil fuels E.g. Recent coal crisis in India. To save electricity defrost the fridge, use compact fluorescents, etc. Not only this but turning off the lights at night or washing clothes in cold water can save trees, coal, natural gas, etc. The least one can do to save water is take a bath using one bucket of water, turn the tap off when not needed & instead of throwing water, feed it to a nearby plant.

Choose products which encourage sustainability. There are products like phone cases which are made from compostable sustainable bio-plastic, reusable coffee cups made out of food grade silicone, mattresses which are certified (certification indicates that foams are made without ozone depleters, without formaldehyde, etc.) or simply opt for latex mattresses which are eco-friendly.

Lifestyle choices which are sustainable and green helps reduce pollution, conserve natural resources, help to lead a healthier life and help one to raise self-aware children. Only through these baby-steps will we be able to preserve our planet whose resources are already depleting. These choices might not be popular, but it is not popularity that always works. By adopting this lifestyle, we will not only help ourselves but also the future generations.

References:

- https://globalecolabelling.net/green-initiatives-and-news/what-is-living
- https://blueandgreentomorrow.com/environment/7-essential-benefits-of-living-green-lifestyle/
- https://www.countryfile.com/green-living/how-to-live-a-greener-life/
- https://www.unep.org/interactives/beat-plastic-pollution/
- https://www.saveonenergy.com/green-energy/save-energy-go-green/
- https://www.onyalife.com/eco-friendly-products/

Approach towards a Greener & Sustainable Lifestyle

XV

Lead the scene and keep it Green. Take a ride on the Green Side.

Ms. Sayed Mohammed Haider Kalbay Asghar

S. Y. B. Ed. Student, Batch 2021-2023
MES's Pillai College of Education and Research
Chembur, Mumbai.

Green living (or sustainable living) is a lifestyle that attempts to reduce an individual's or society's use of the Earth's natural resources and his or her own resources. In practice, it deals about practical lifestyle choices, large and small, to live in line with the Earth's carrying capacities, while maintaining (or sometimes improving) our quality of life. Besides lifestyle choices, the housing and appliances we use also has its impact on the environment. .

Practitioners of sustainable living often attempt to reduce their carbon footprint by altering methods of transportation, energy consumption and diet. Proponents of sustainable living aim to conduct their lives in ways that are consistent with sustainability, in natural balance and respectful of humanity's symbiotic relationship with the Earth's natural ecology and cycles. The practice and general philosophy of ecological living is highly interrelated with the overall principles of sustainable development.

Today, more and more companies are creating products that help us live a green lifestyle. Everything from cars, light bulbs, utensils, straws, cleaners, mattresses, and clothing is created with environmental preservation in mind. These products help us conserve water, energy and precious natural resources while also helping to curb pollution. The convenience these products provide make it easier than ever to live sustainably

The choices which we make to go green has a huge impact on environment one can start it from oneself by taking many steps

1. Reduction of meat consumption.
2. Using Public transport or electrical vehicle.
3. 3 R Mantra Reduce, Reuse, Recycle.
4. Buying or producing one's own energy.

Healthier Foods: When we choose to make more eco-friendly food choices such as buying local, organic, and seasonal foods, we are supporting sustainable farming methods that protect our planet. In turn, these methods help reduce the number of harmful pesticides that end up in our food. Research shows that exposure to pesticides can antagonize the natural hormones in our bodies, leading to health issues such as immune suppression, hormone disruption, reproductive abnormalities, and cancer.

Save Money: Conserving water and energy will not only help us save natural resources, but it will also help us save money. Using energy-efficient appliances and LED light bulbs in the home can also cut up to 30 percent off our annual electricity bill. That's an average of $627 per year depending on the appliance, home, and climate.

Curb Climate Change: The burning of fossil fuels for energy is one of the biggest contributors to climate change. This type of energy results in destructive carbon dioxide emissions that pollute our environment. One way individuals can help to combat climate change is to reduce our energy consumption. Research shows that switching to energy-efficient appliances could help to reduce carbon emissions by up to 19 percent. In 2017, recycling alone saved over 184 million tons of carbon dioxide from our environment. This is the equivalent of removing 39 million cars from the road in one year. Taking steps to conserve energy in our homes can go a long way in reducing carbon emissions and protecting our planet for future generations.

It is more important than ever to adopt a green lifestyle. These small changes can help reduce the pollution that threatens our health and our environment, while also protecting our natural resources. Fortunately, it has never been easier to live a sustainable lifestyle.

Energy-efficient appliances are more affordable than ever, recycling is available in most Indian cities, and many companies are creating convenient products using eco-friendly practices and materials. When we all take small steps toward preserving our planet, we all reap big rewards.